The Thing About
STRESS

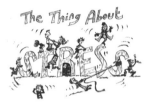

Published by
Lion Publishing plc
Mayfield House, 256 Banbury Road,
Oxford OX2 7DH, England
www.lion-publishing.co.uk
ISBN 0 7459 4629 1

First edition 2002
10 9 8 7 6 5 4 3 2 1

Acknowledgments

14, 72: Proverbs 14:30, Proverbs 17:6, taken from the *Holy Bible*, New Living Translation,
copyright © 1996. Used by permission of Tyndale House Publishers, Inc., Wheaton, Illinois
60189. All rights reserved. 52, 65, 70: Matthew 16:26, 1 Timothy 6:10, Proverbs 17:6, taken
from the *Holy Bible, New International Version*, copyright © 1973, 1978, 1984 by International
Bible Society. Used by permission.

A catalogue record for this book is available
from the British Library

Typeset in Humanist 521
Printed and bound in Malta

The Thing About STRESS

Written by Liz Babbs

Illustrated by Kate Sheppard

LION
Giftlines

So you're stressed

Take time to rest

Relax and unwind

Establish boundaries

Surrender control

Search for balance

Stress-Busters ••••••••••••••••••••••

Stress is... having
too many self-help books
and no time to read any
of them!

Time Out

Life is not a race to the finish, it's a journey. So don't worry and hurry your way through. Take your time and enjoy it.

Research shows that we do our best thinking during periods of reflection rather than activity.

Time is the most valuable resource you have. The way you spend it determines your quality of life, so manage it carefully.

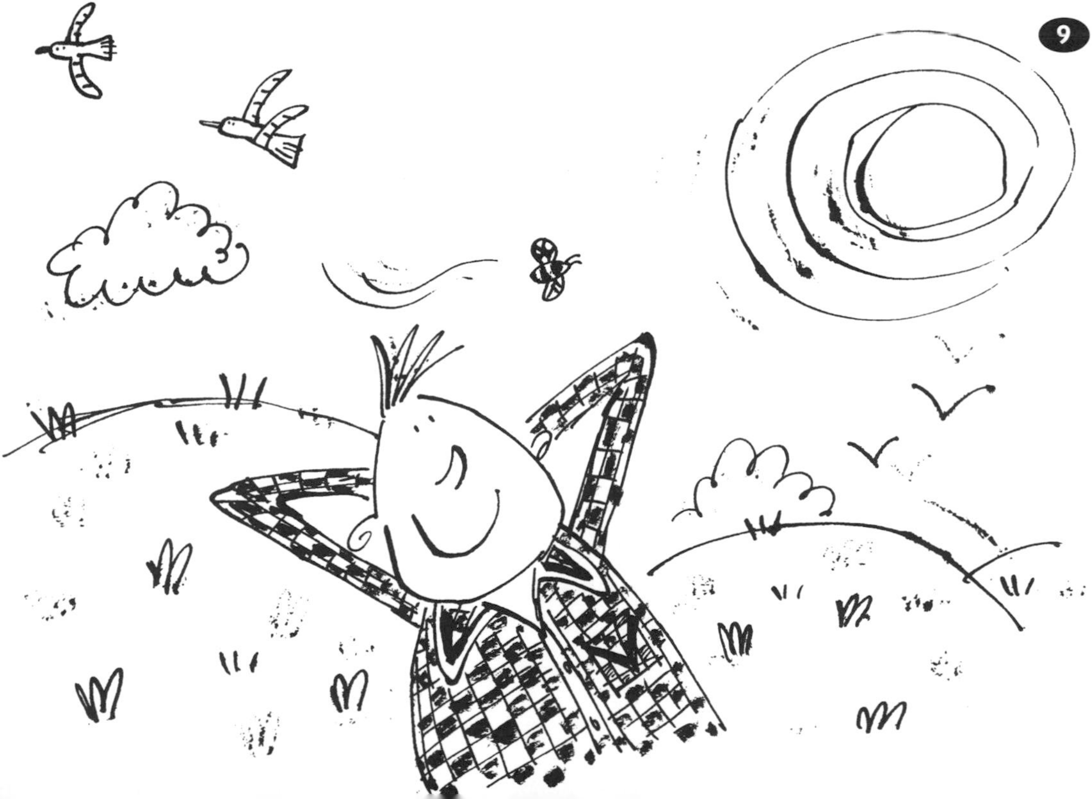

• • • • • • • • • • • • • • • •

Come apart and
take time out
before you come
a...p...a...r...t!

**Don't run yourself
ragged doing
everything yourself.
Ask for help.**

Burnout
is your divine opportunity
to take stock and sort out your
priorities before it's too late.

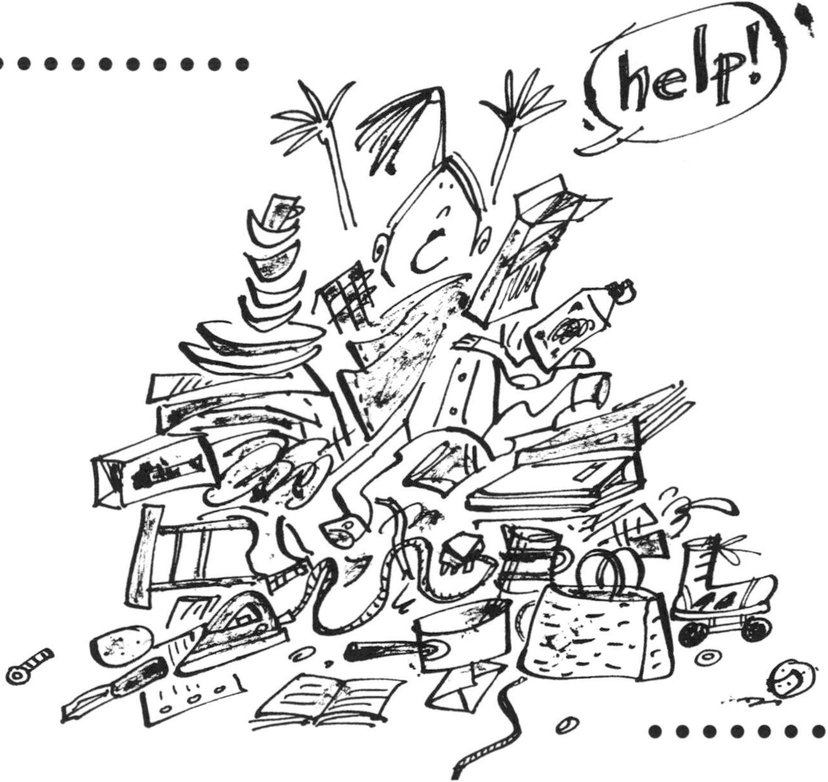
help!

When you value your leisure time as much as your work time, you'll be surprised by the difference it makes.

Music is deeply relaxing. Allow it to be your 'voice of the soul'.

Life is a series of choices, so don't feel guilty about taking time to enjoy yourself.

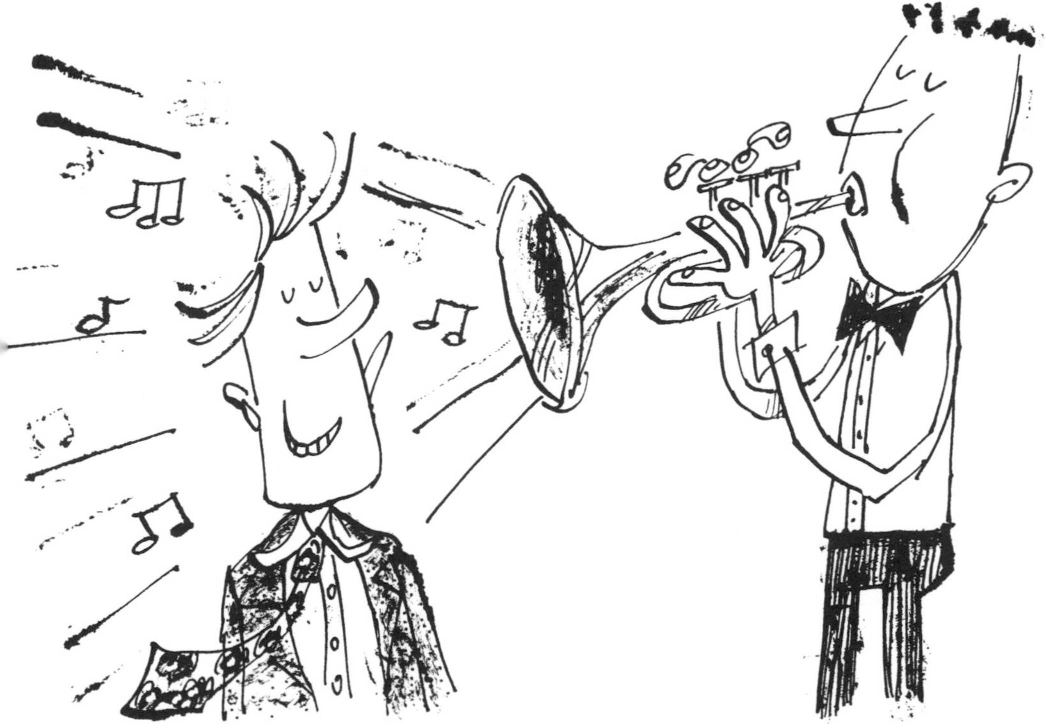

To make the most of your 'time out' socializing, make sure that you have spent enough 'time in' resting and recharging your batteries.

A
relaxed attitude
lengthens life.

The Bible

Fast food = indigestion! Don't rush to eat your lunch. Eating is one of life's pleasures. Sit down, relax, and enjoy it.

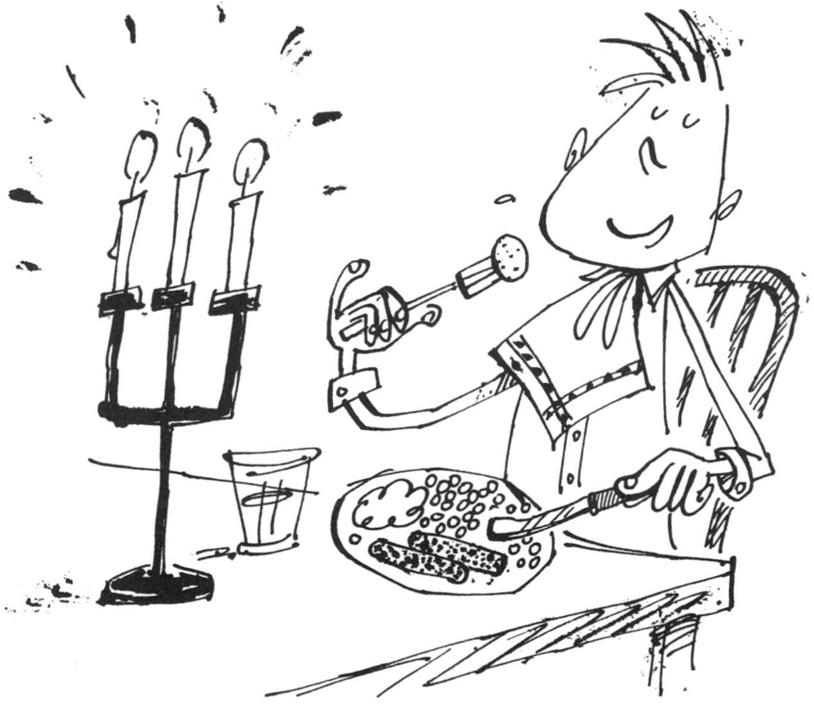

• • • • • • • • • • • • • • • • • • • •

Live in the present
and don't dwell on
the past or the future.
You'll have enough to
deal with tomorrow.

To
'be' or to 'do' is a
question of choice.

**Doing nothing is
not a waste of time,
but an investment
of time.**

• • • • • • • • • • • • • •

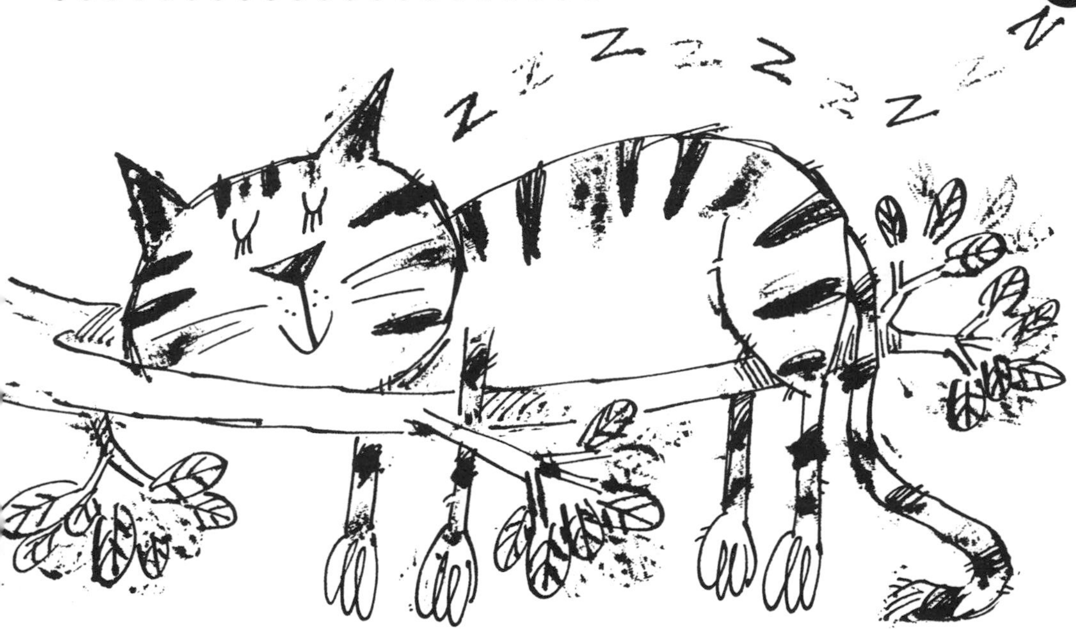

Similarities between
you and your computer:
both crash when
overloaded!

Work Out

• • • • • • • • • • • • • • • • • • • •

It has been said that life is 10% what happens to you and 90% how you respond.

> Work is only a pressure if you do too much of it.

The greatest cause of overload is the inability to say no. Respect your health and don't be a people-pleaser.

• • • • • • • • • • • • • • • • • • • •

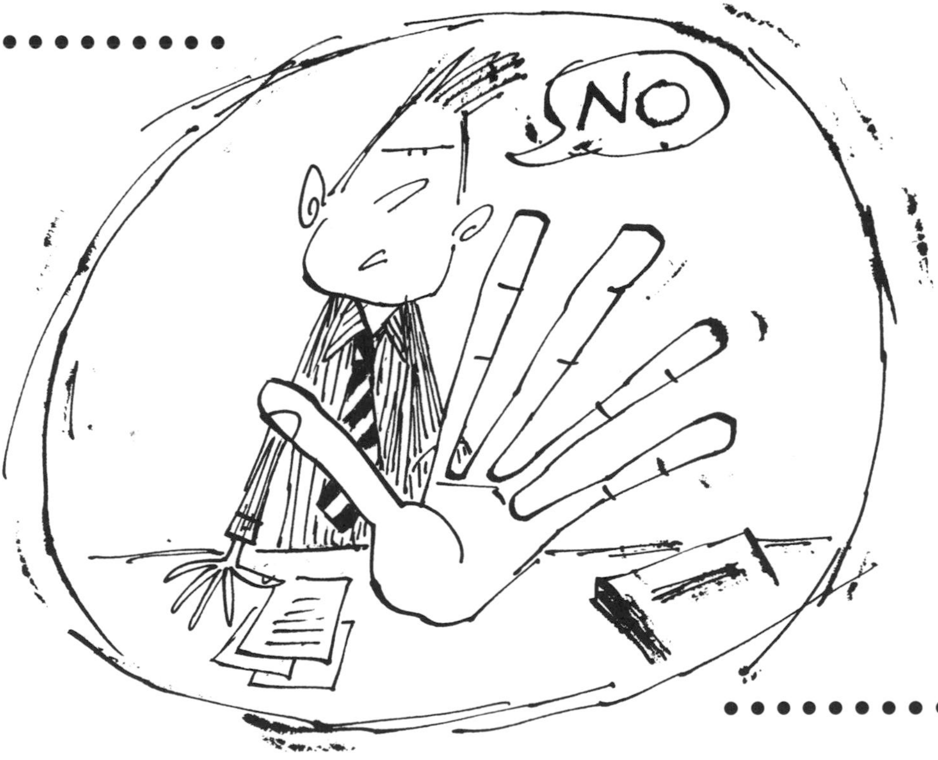
NO

• • • • • • • • • • • • • • • • • • •

Work always expands
to fill the time available,
so prioritize leisure time
by planning it into your
diary.

When you visit
the gym, make sure
you're not swapping
one treadmill for
another.

It is a false economy to
work continuously. Regular breaks
fuel greater productivity and
creativity.

• • • • • • • • • • • • • • •

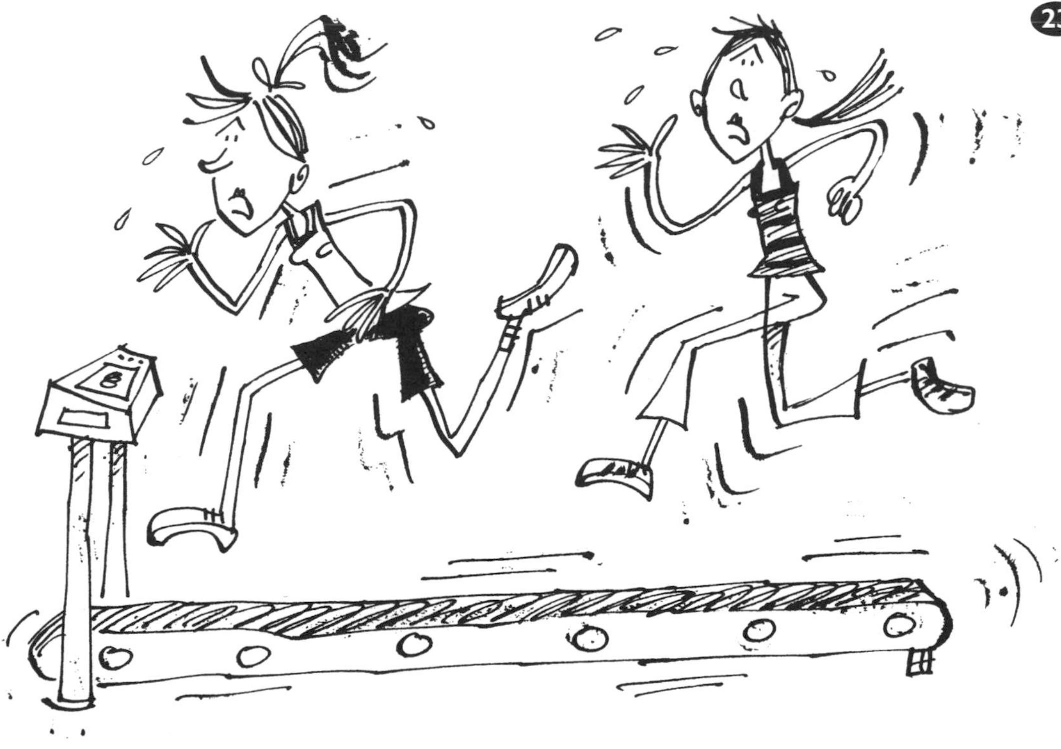

It's not the problem that's the issue, it's how you handle the problem.

As pressure at work increases, you have a choice: learn to manage it, or let it manage you!

Don't you long for a message like this? 'Hi there, this is God here. I'm going to be handling all your problems today, so don't worry, put your feet up and let me take care of everything for you.'

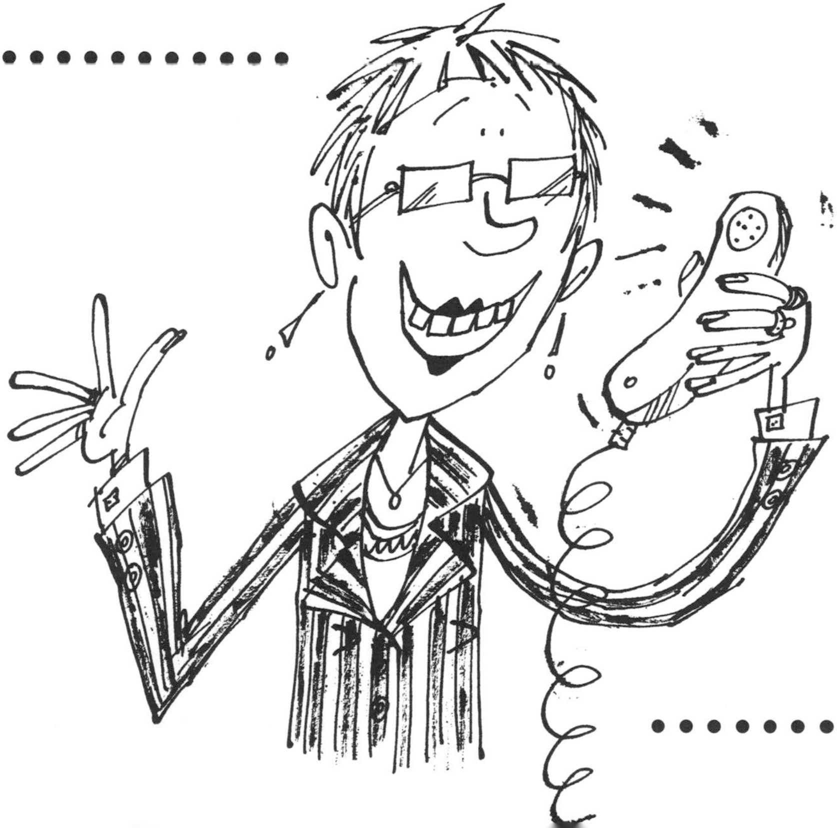

If you're struggling and labouring over something without success, check that your 'good idea' really is a good idea.

Poor choices lead to poor outcomes.

Avoid taking your work home with you. Relaxation and recreation are important too.

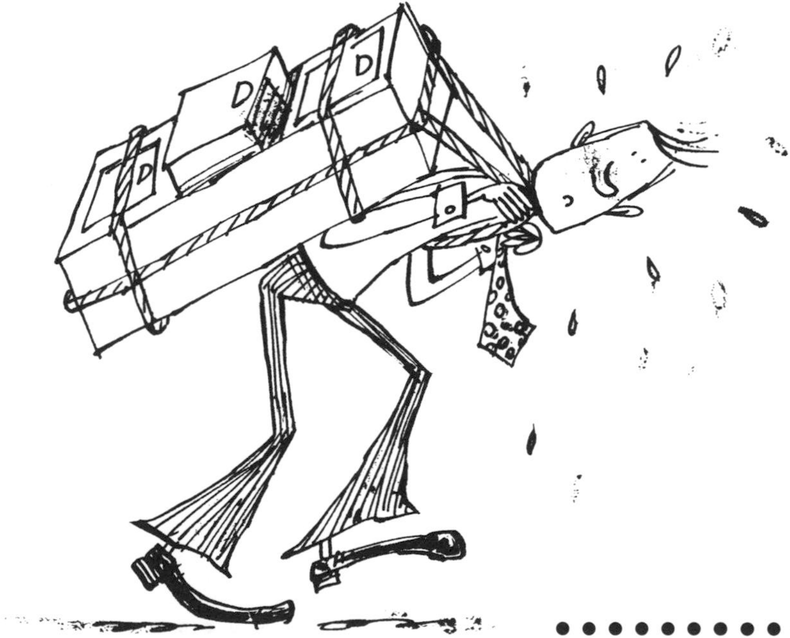

Don't worry about your problems. Problems are only solutions waiting to happen.

Don't compare yourself with other people. Set realistic but challenging personal goals instead.

Words are containers of power, so watch negative self-talk.

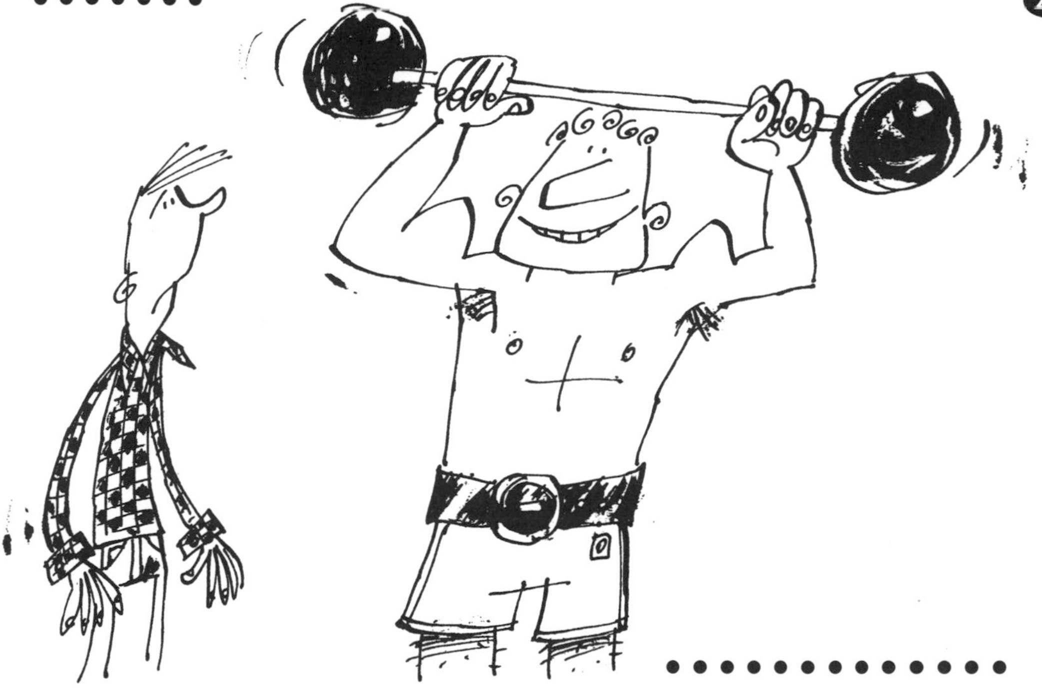

•••••••••••••••••••••

Accept change as a challenge, not a threat. Discuss your feelings openly with others, and try to maximize potential gains and minimize losses.

Confront your fears and they will lose their power. Ask yourself, 'What is the worst thing that could happen?'

The problems we encounter are our greatest opportunity for growth.

•••••••••••••••

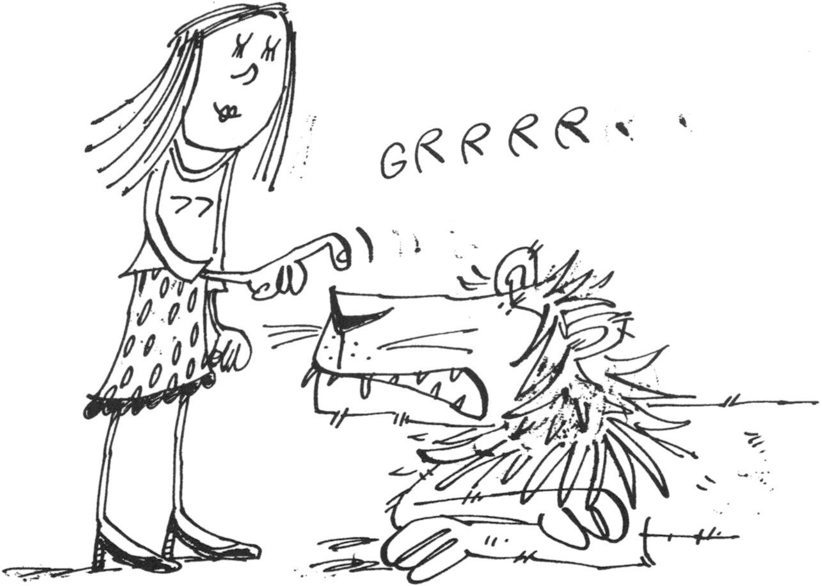
GRRRRR

Don't have so many irons in the fire that you put it out!

Chill Out

Stress can seriously
damage your health,
so take it seriously.

If you were to live each
day as though it were your
last, your priorities would
soon change.

Laughter is a great
medicine: it promotes
healing and reduces
stress. Seek out
friends who make
you laugh, go to the
cinema or have a
store of your favourite
comedies on video.

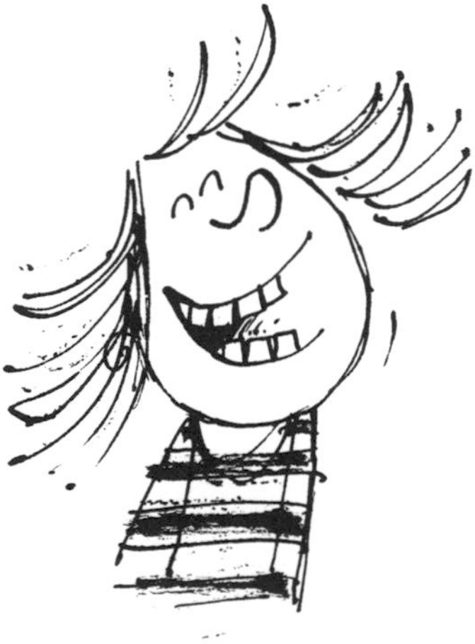

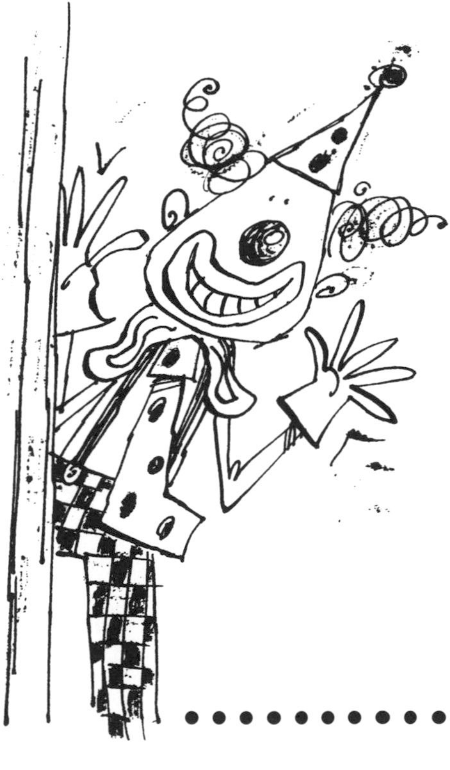

Exhaustion is a great place to learn your limitations and the need to pace yourself.

Allowing enough time for your body to recover after exercise is part of fitness too.

Research shows that guilt can weaken the immune system, making it harder to fight infection.

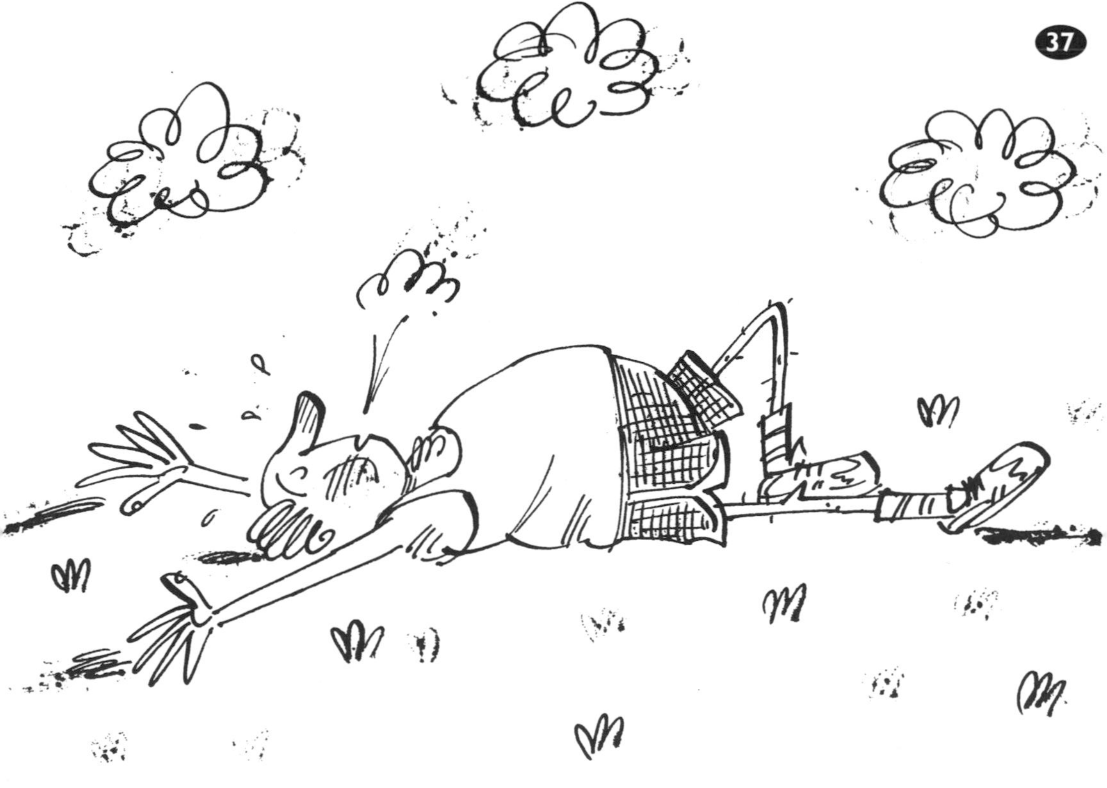

• • • • • • • • • • • • • • • • • • •

Rest is not just a four-letter word — it is vital to your health and well-being.

De-stress by regularly treating yourself to a long soothing aromatic bath or massage.

Meditation and prayer are not only natural stress-busters, but they help you to be more at peace with yourself, with others and with God.

• • • • • • • • • • • • • • •

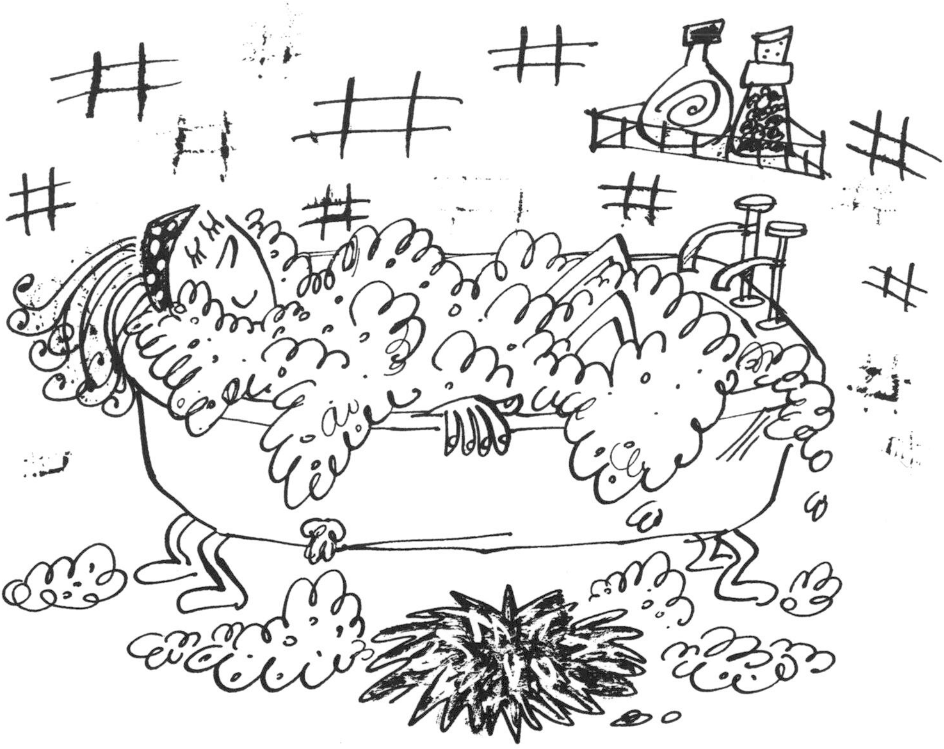

Your body is a spiritual vessel, so treat yourself with reverence and respect.

Fear drives but love leads, so look at your reasons for 'doing' and 'overdoing' things.

Stress leads to shallow breathing. Relaxed breathing is slow and stomach-centred, using the diaphragm. Try to recognize when your breathing is shallow, adjust your posture and breathe in deeply and slowly.

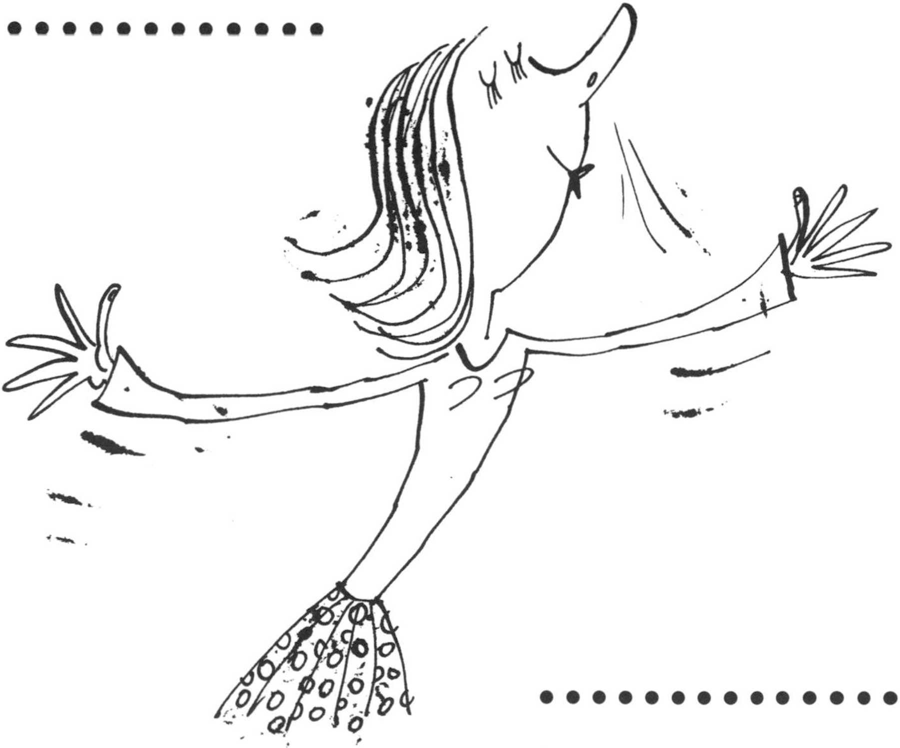

A balanced diet will give you more energy, strengthen your immune system and lift your mood.

Exercise is a great way to release anger and frustration. It also increases the production of feel-good endorphins.

Frowning causes more age lines than smiling, so you might as well relax and smile!

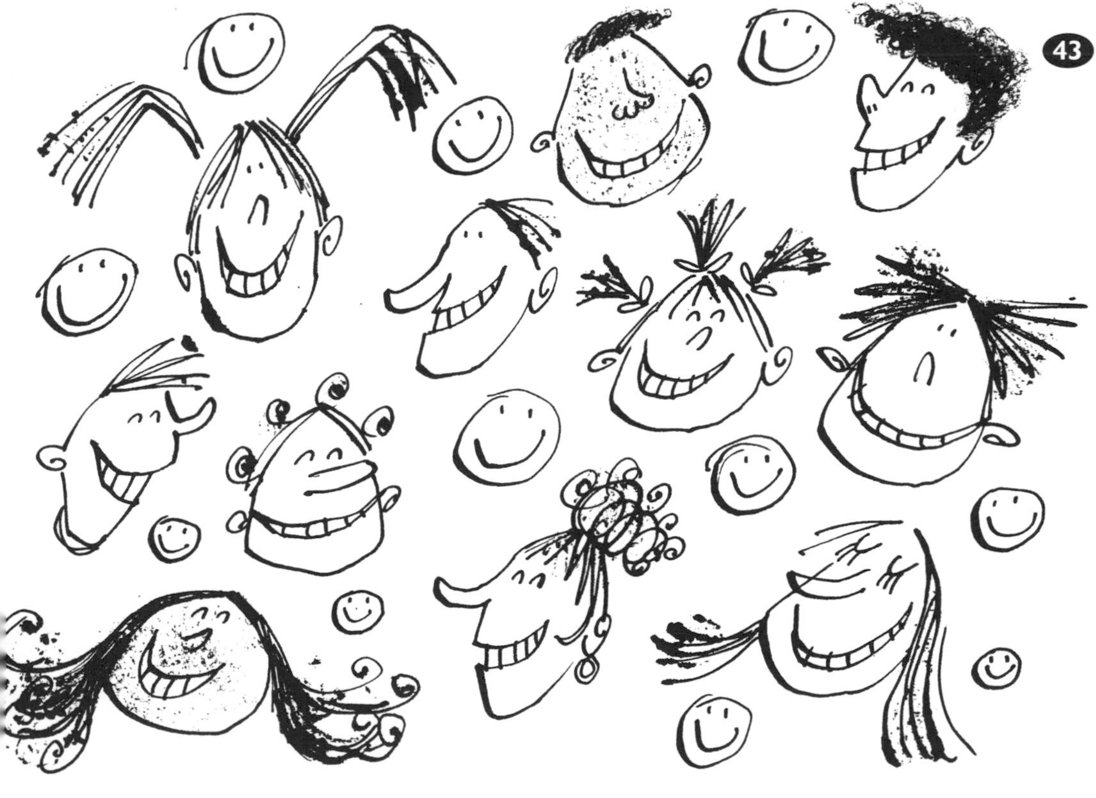

Cultivate silence. It will heighten your awareness and appreciation of everything around you.

Go for a countryside walk, visit an empty church or place of pilgrimage and savour the peace and stillness.

Getting enough sleep is the most important factor in preventing fatigue.

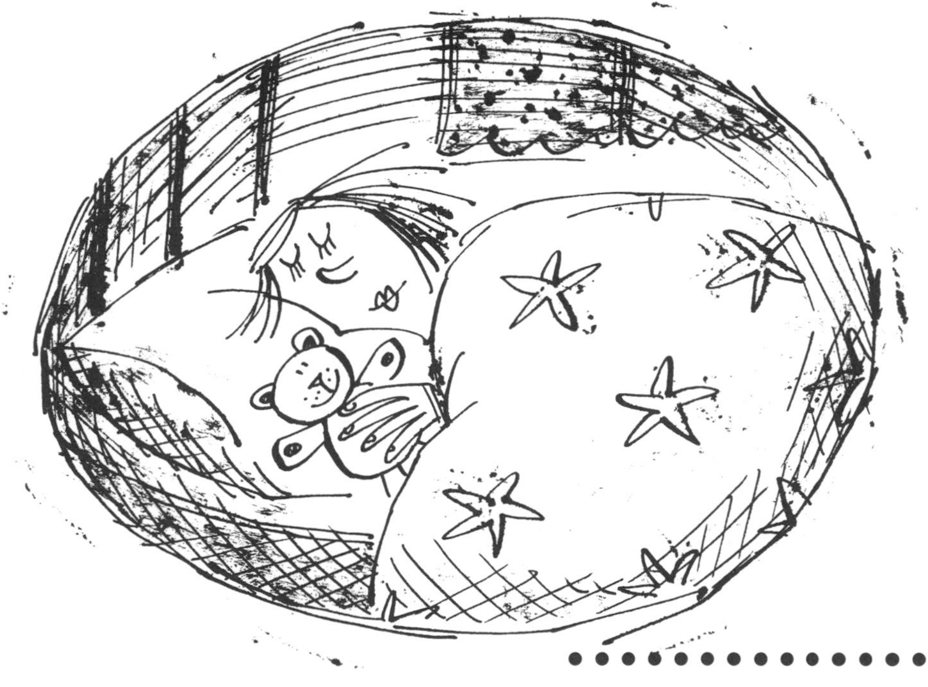

Don't sweep your health problems under the carpet with painkillers, face up to them.

Laugh a lot. It not only relieves tension, but tightens tummy muscles too!

Cut down on 'mood food' such as salt, sugar, caffeine and alcohol. Eaten in excess, they affect your stress levels.

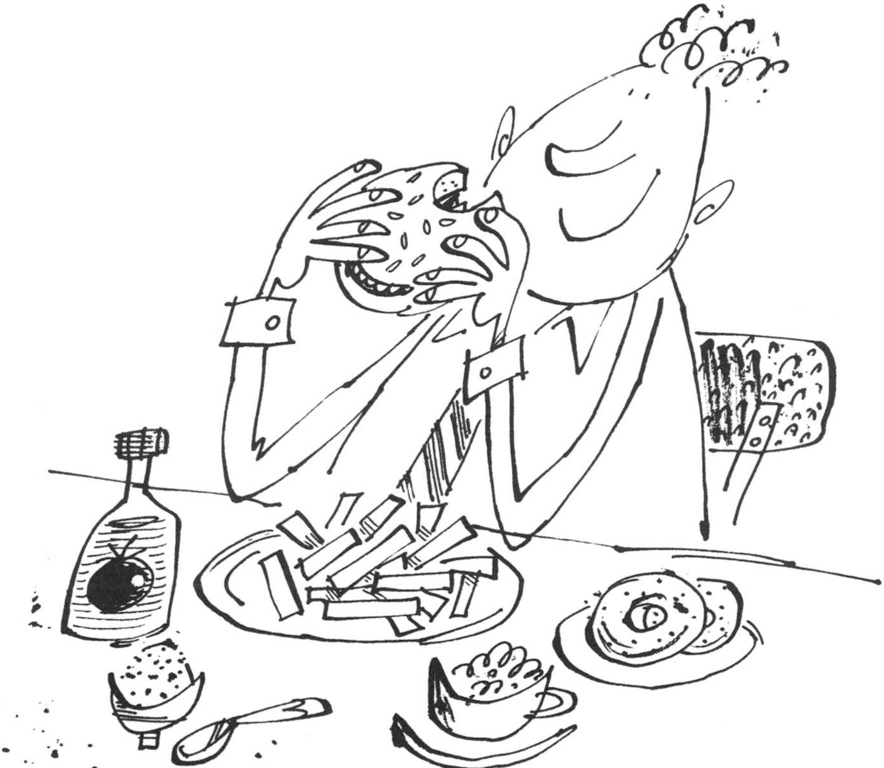

Strife is like a cancer —
it's progressive. Deal with it
before it consumes you.

Don't
let your feelings have
the final vote.

If at first you don't succeed... try exercise or a little chocolate! Research shows that they both reduce anxiety levels.

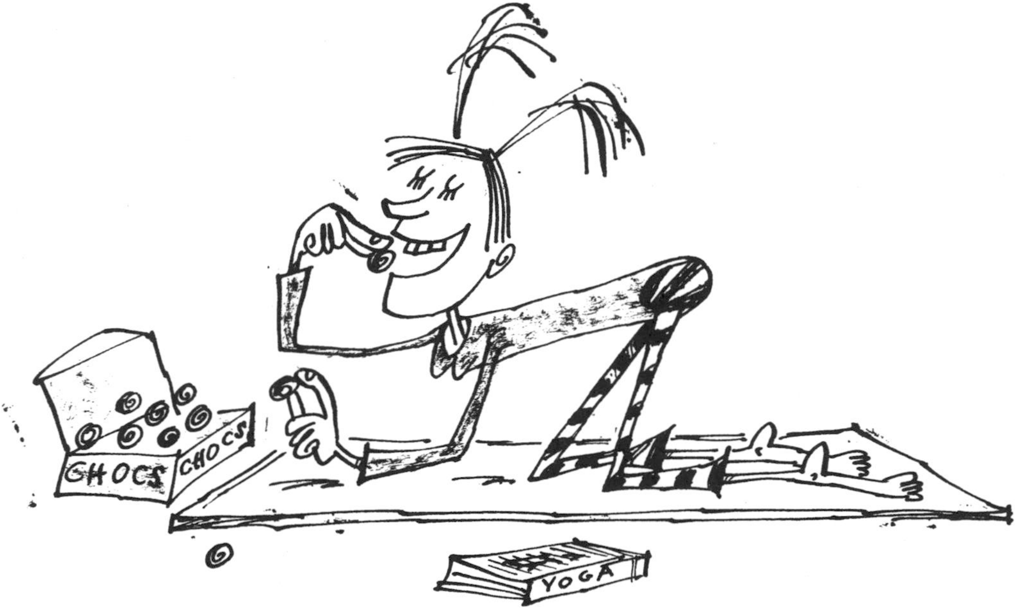
CHOCS
CHOCS
YOGA

Don't worry about tomorrow. Tomorrow will have enough shopping hours of its own!

Money Matters

No amount of money, fame or power can replace a friend.

Don't spend in a day what you earn in a month.

What good will it be for a man if he gains the whole world, yet forfeits his soul?

The Bible

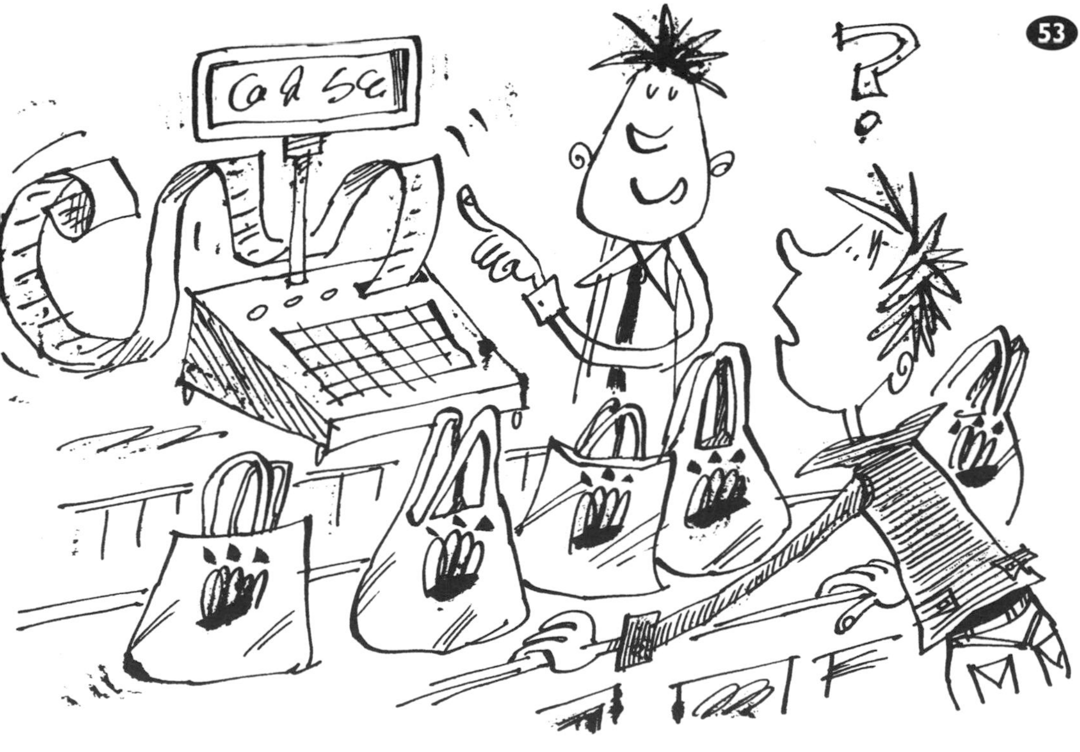

Sort out your debts before you save, or you'll always struggle to pay what you owe.

Leave your plastic at home. Handling cash will make you more aware of what you are spending.

The only difference between an optimist and a pessimist is what they choose to focus on.

• • • • • • • • • • • • • • •

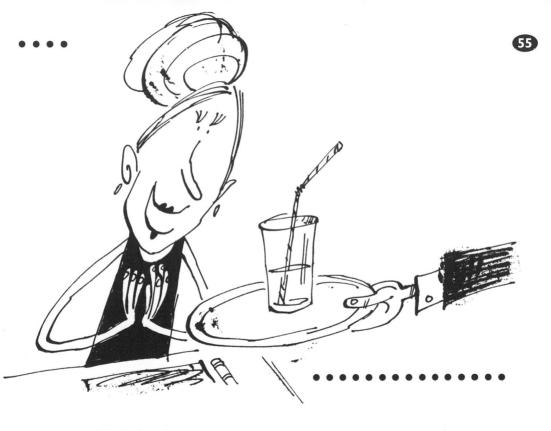

Before buying an expensive item, do your homework and check whether you can afford it.

Stress is... not telling your partner what you've spent until they see the bank overdraft statement.

In money terms, your children are worth everything.

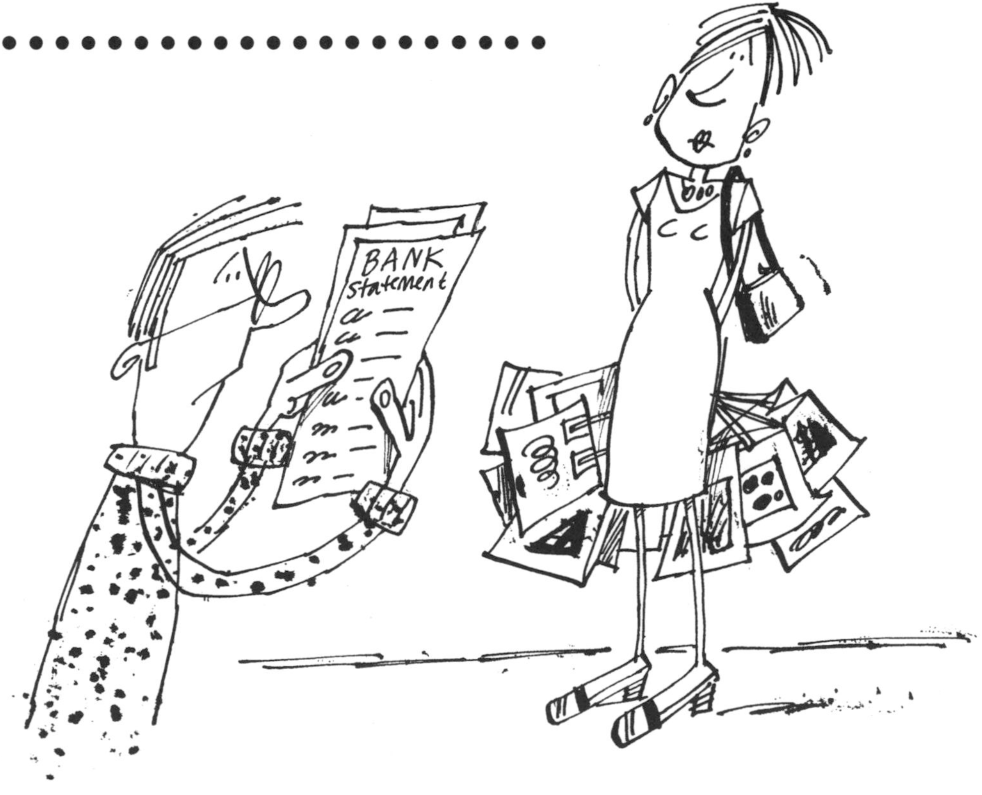
BANK
statement

Over-spending can
seriously damage your health,
not just your wealth.

**Don't be pressurized
by sales people into
borrowing more than
you can afford.**

*Money changes people,
so treat it with respect.*

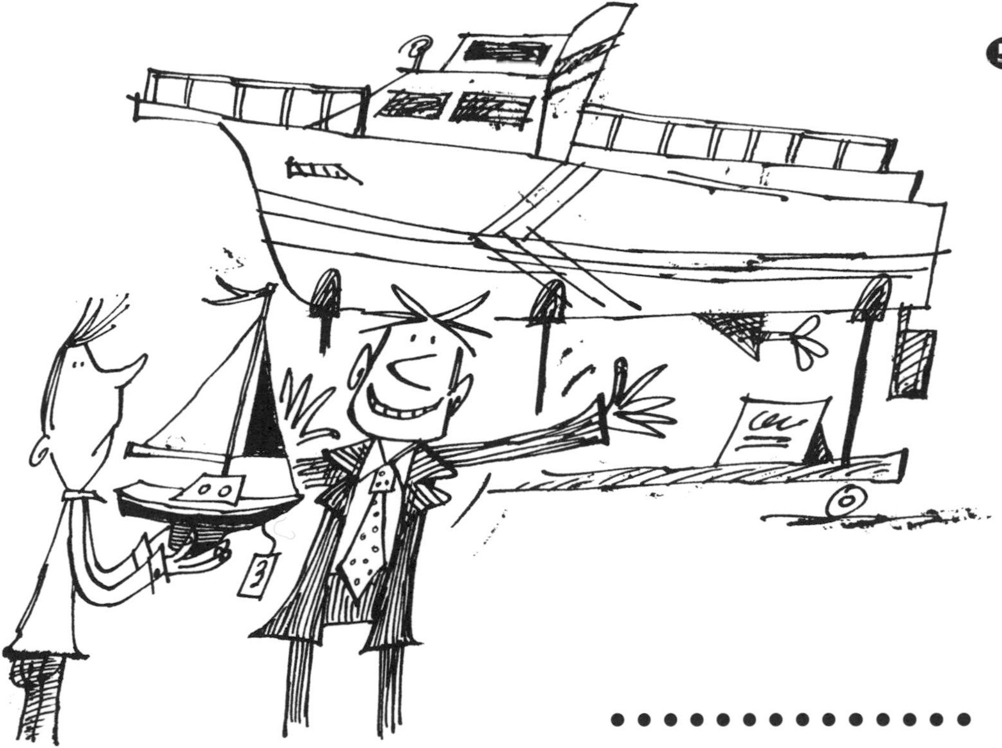
3

Shopping may be a necessity, but retail therapy can be fun.

Charity may be said to begin at home, but it doesn't have to stay there!

For every person who wins a million, there are millions who don't.

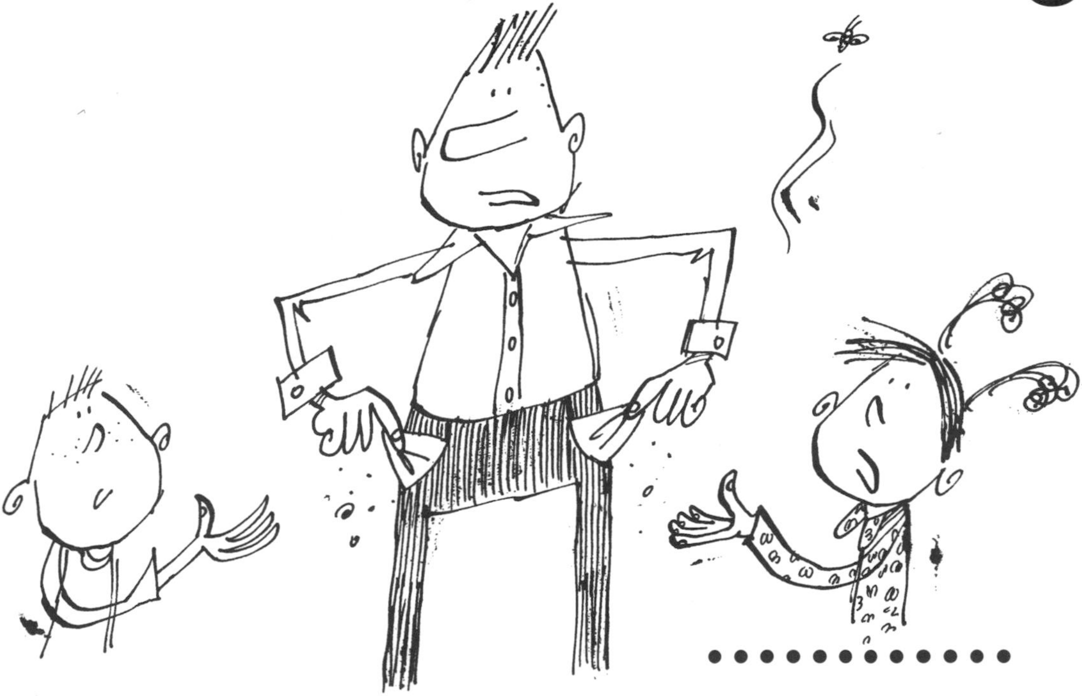

Shares
may have little to do with
sharing and a lot to do with
greed.

**Watch that your
credit cards don't
take charge of
your life.**

Good health is more
important than sudden
wealth.

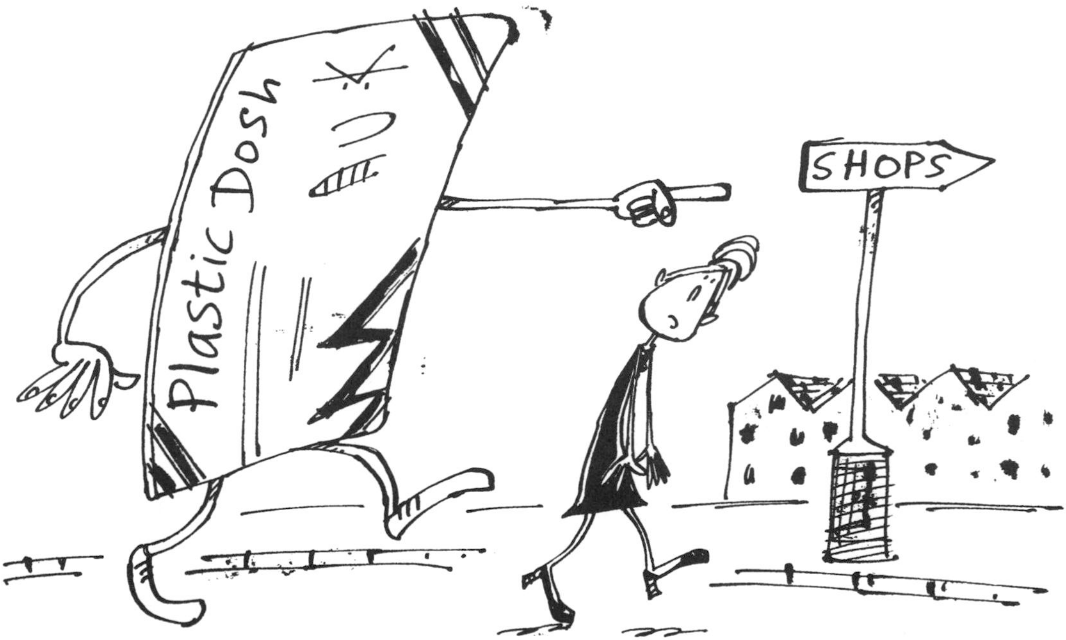
Plastic Dosh
SHOPS

Debt problems can become serious if you ignore them. Take action before it's too late.

Face up to your debts by making a list of income and expenditure. Then budget accordingly.

If you're too busy to sort out your finances... you're too busy!

Don't put off until tomorrow what you need to face up to today.

The love of money is a root of all kinds of evil.

The Bible

Teenagers
+
Hormones
= STRESS!

Family Matters

Nothing is more important than the people you love. Don't let your busyness take you away from your loved ones.

Does your home reflect your lifestyle? Don't let the state of your house become another stress factor.

Live each day for what you can give, rather than for what you can get out of it.

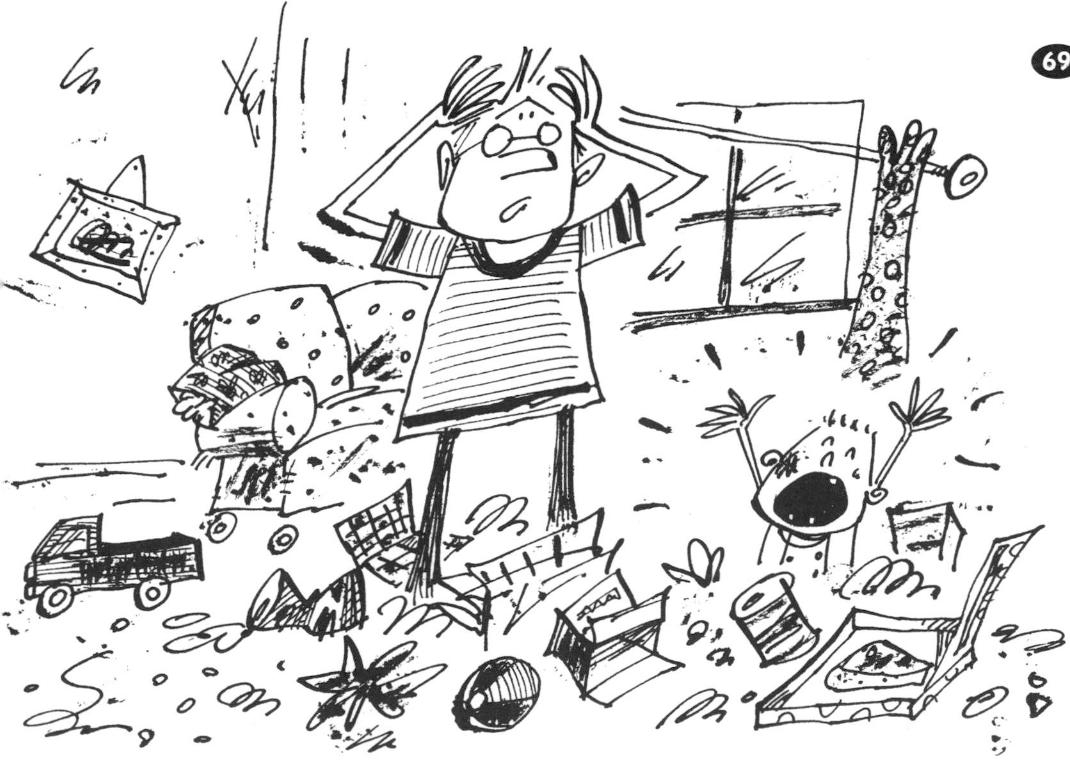

Parents are the pride
of their children.

The Bible

There's
no such thing
as the perfect
parent, but a little
love always goes
a long way.

Make time for your children. They need you more than your presents.

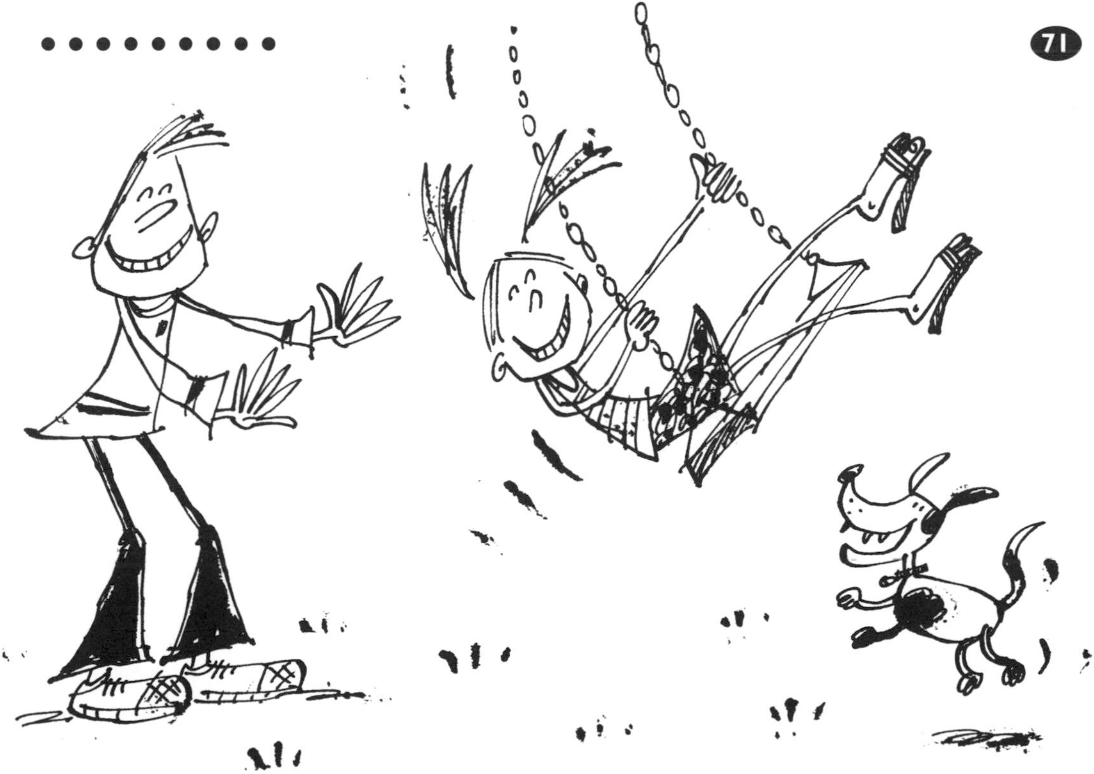

To have a sister is
to have a friend for life.

**Grandchildren are
the crowning glory
of the aged.**

The Bible

Forgiveness is
the key to unlocking
broken relationships.

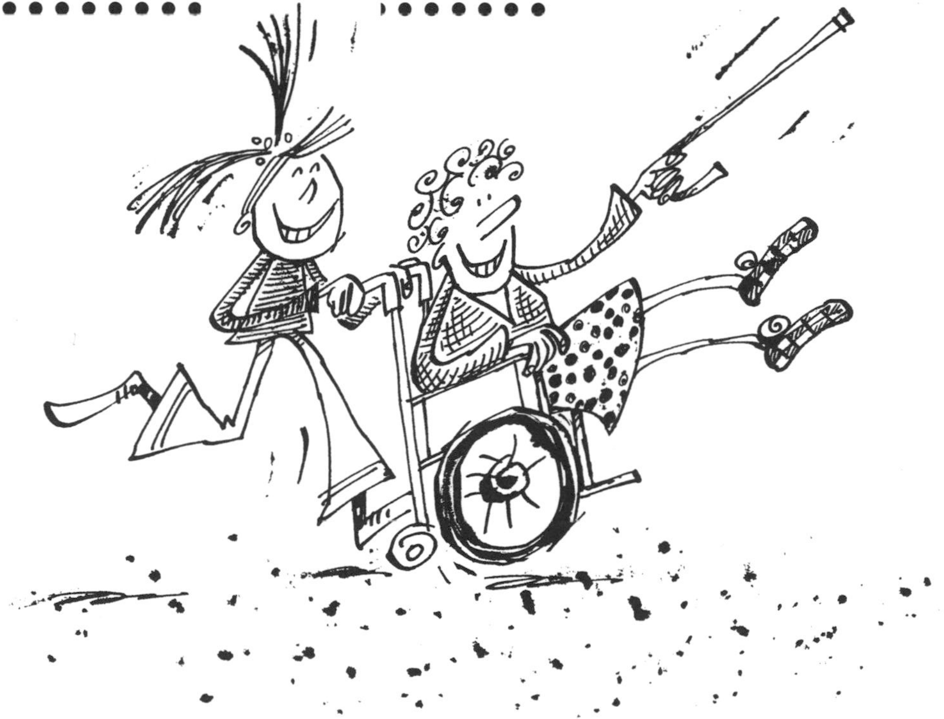

Don't let your children control you. Set boundaries and negotiate limits.

There are some things that only a sister can tell you.

Friends come and go, but a mother is for life.

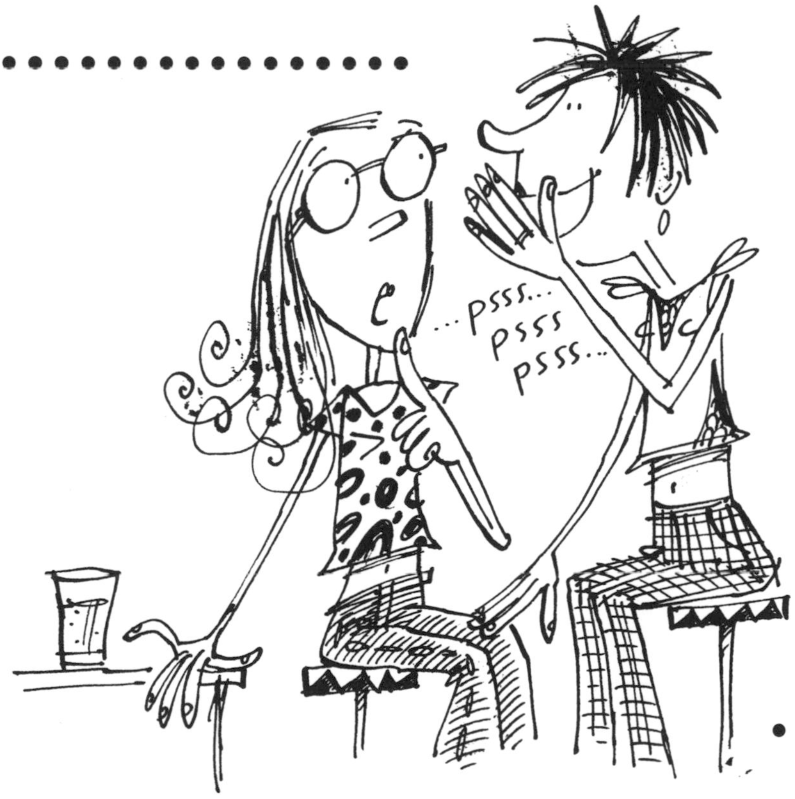
...psss...
psss
psss...

Children are more likely to cooperate if they feel they've been listened to.

Stress is... discovering that this year's Christmas presents were last year's 'must-have' craze!

Value your teenagers as much as they value your money!

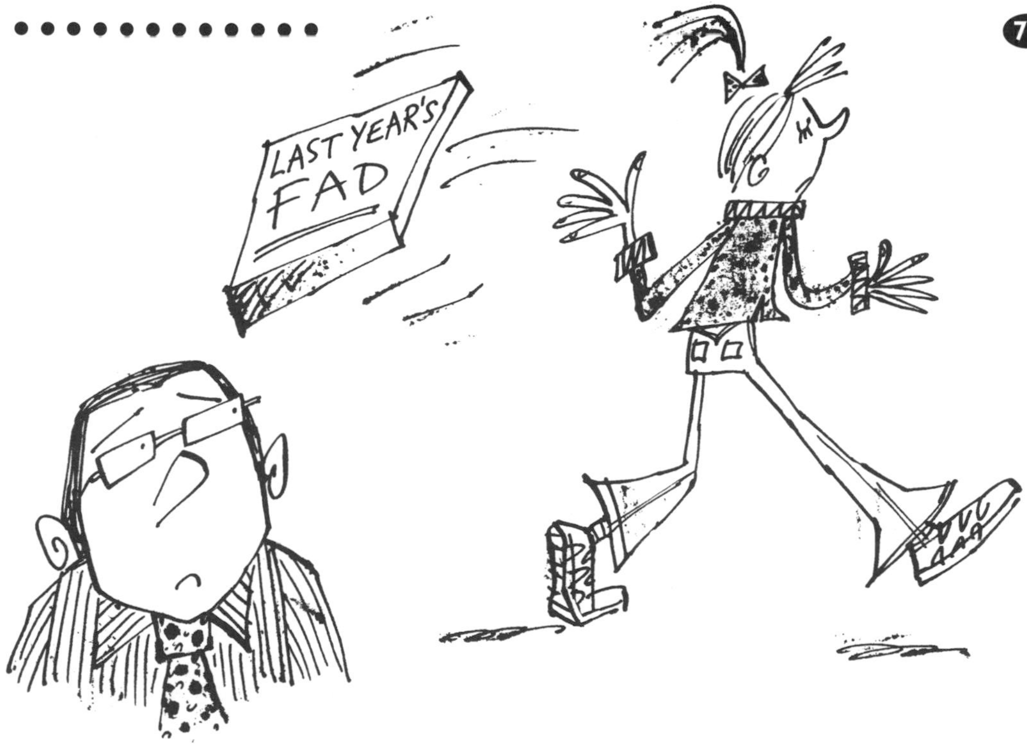
LAST YEAR'S FAD

Don't feel guilty about not spending enough time with your children. It's the quality of the time that counts.

Have a quiet day. Switch your phone off, don't answer the door, forget the chores and enjoy silence and solitude – it's deeply healing.

Don't worry if your youngsters say 'I'm bored.' Research shows that boredom can be good for the imagination.

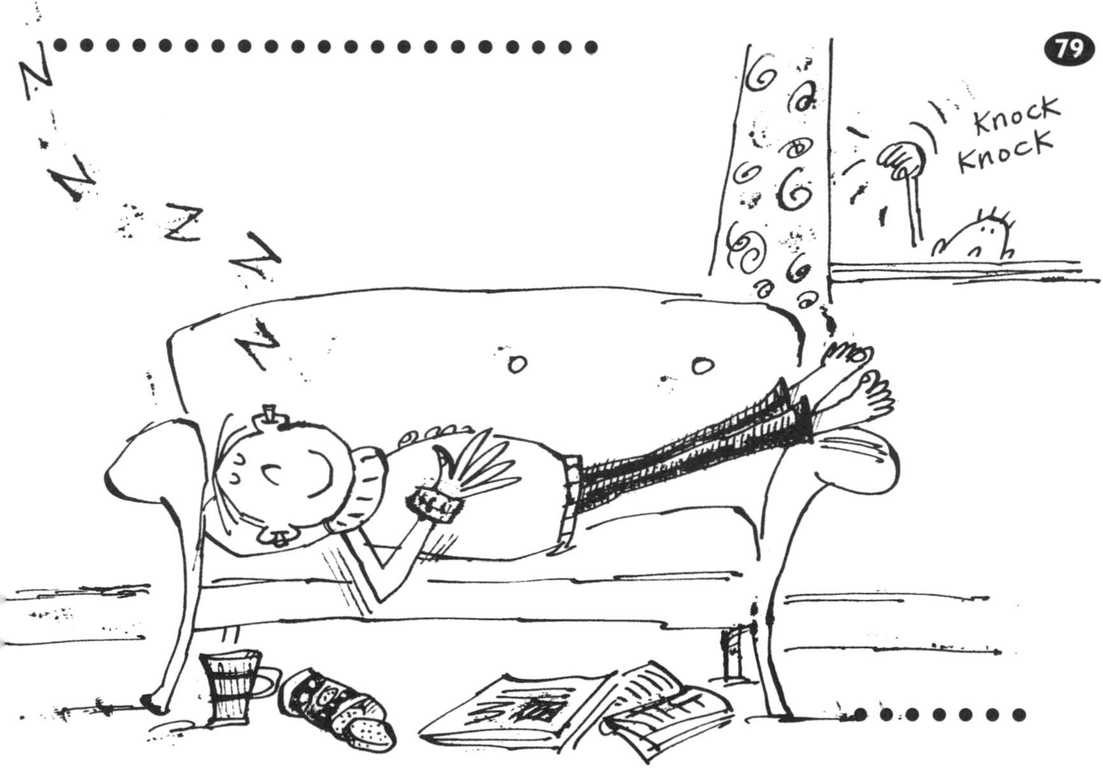
Knock
Knock

**Loving discipline
is not the same as
child abuse.**

'Chill out' with your
kids. Research shows
that over-stimulation
reduces creativity.

A family that
eats together
meets together.

Don't look to another person to complete you. One person cannot meet all your needs.

When your youngsters demand things immediately, choose not to get wound up, then prioritize according to urgency and importance.

Life is what
happens when you
have something
else planned.

Relationship Issues

Love is not performance-related, it's unconditional.

Suppressed anger leads to tension and bitterness. Own your feelings, express them appropriately and then forgive.

Some people go into a relationship looking for a bargain. But if you give little, you'll receive little. So give generously!

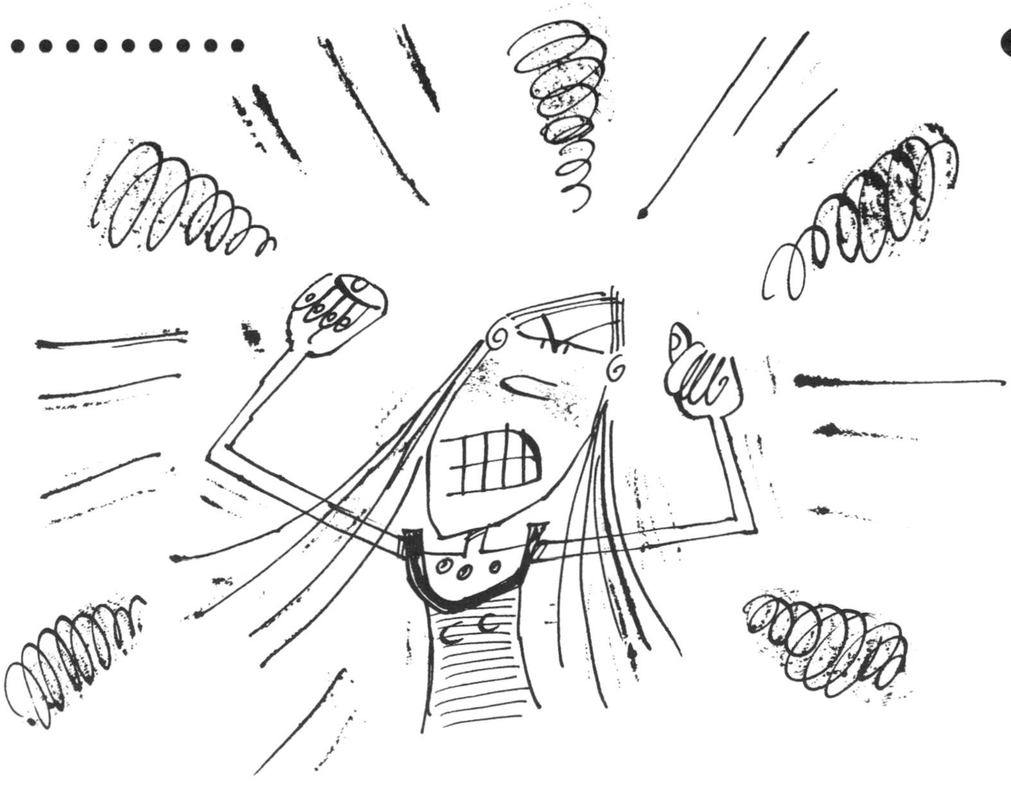

Don't bottle everything up.
Give your feelings a voice.

Apathy won't solve your
problems, but cultivating
a passion for something
may well do.

It's important to
give to those in need,
but remember, not
every need should
be met by you!

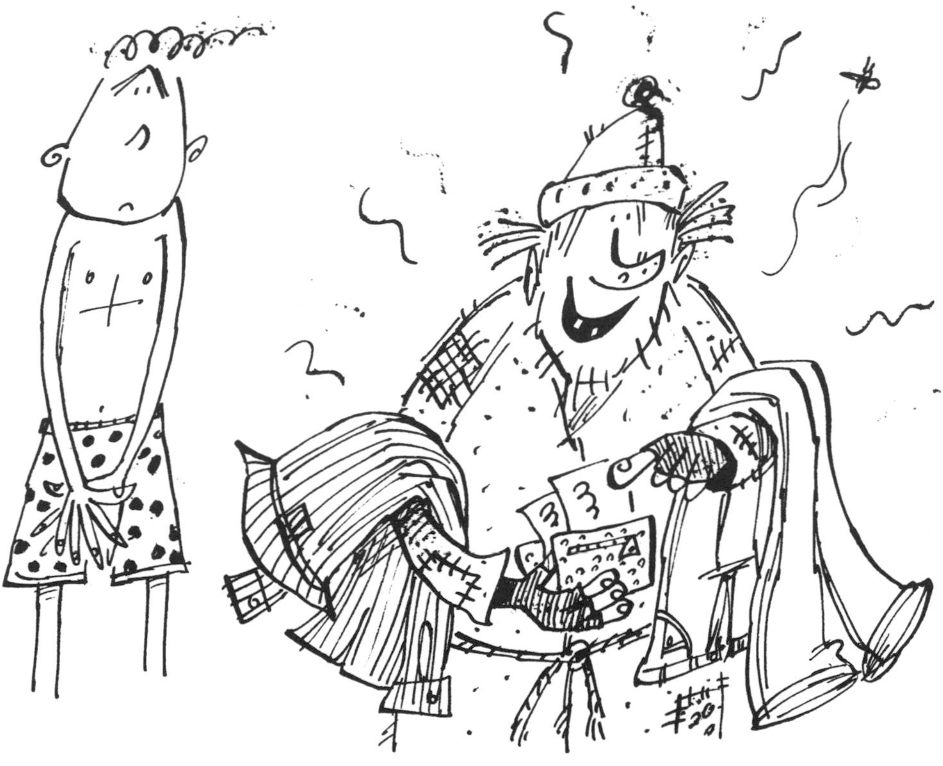

Beauty really does come from within, so guard your heart – it affects everything you say, think and do.

Don't shoot your mouth off before listening to the facts.

Remember to give and receive compliments with grace.

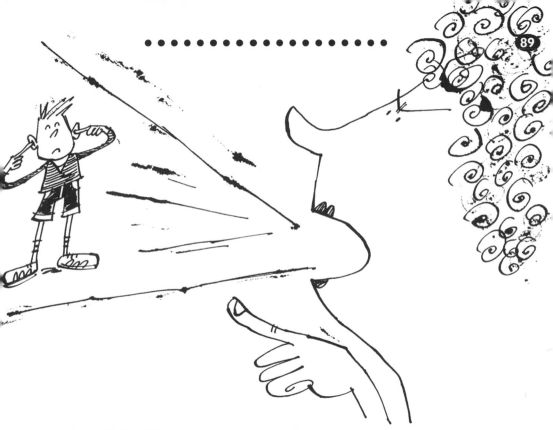

Communication oils the
wheels of friendship.

De-junk your life.
Holding on to the
past can stifle the
present.

Asking for help
is a sign of wisdom,
not weakness.

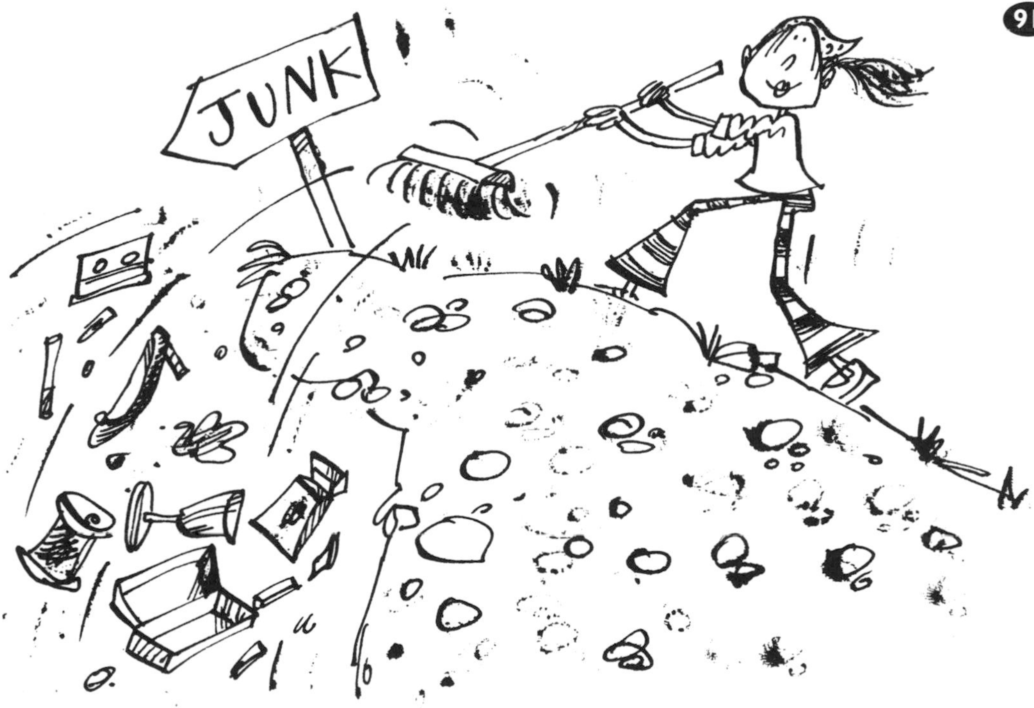
JUNK

Relationships are managed, not cured. Don't try and fix your partner, but discuss your needs openly with each other.

Don't overburden friends with your feelings. Try writing things down instead.

Unrealistic expectations of other people only lead to disappointment. Expect less and you'll be pleasantly surprised.

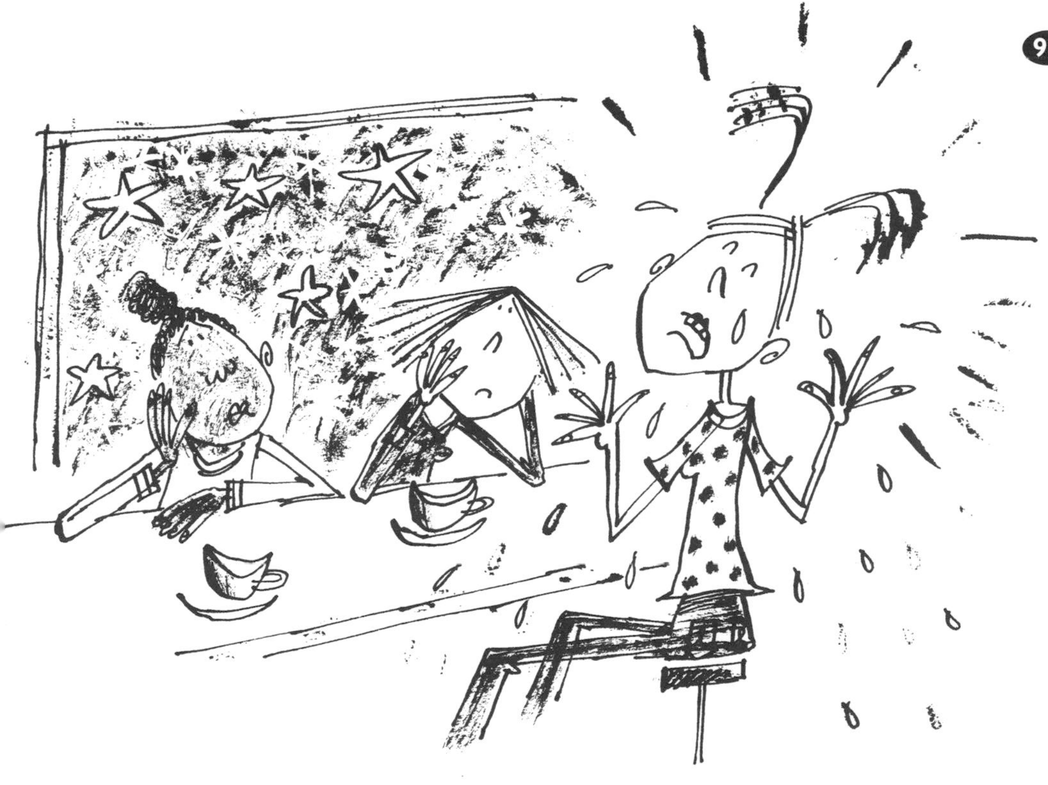

Our enemies highlight our weaknesses. When caught in conflict try asking yourself, 'What is this showing me about myself?'

Tell the truth. A lie creates a jagged edge that's difficult to heal.

To resolve a problem you have to address it.

- **B**elieve in yourself
- **E**liminate negative self-talk
- **L**earn to love yourself
- **I**nvest your time wisely
- **E**liminate perfectionist tendencies
- **V**alue your family and friends
- **E**stablish good principles for living

Love is a risk that only brave people take.

● ●

> **You can contact the author**
> **via her web page:**
>
> **www.lizbabbs.com**

● ● ● ● ● ● ● ● ● ● ● ● ● ● ●